AN INSIDER'S GUIDE TO NON-QM

AUDIO BOOKS

— your best choice —

Download the Audiobook FREE!

Just to say thank you for buying my book, I would like to give you the audiobook FREE!

To download, go to:

http://non-qminsider.com/freebook

AN INSIDER'S GUIDE TO

NON-QM

A Mortgage Loan Orginator's Guide to Bigger Paychecks In a Declining Mortgage Market

Fernando Zoota

Cover Design: Fernando Zoota

Dad, you're literally one in a million. I'm lucky to have you as a Father.

Mom, you're a rock. Our family wouldn't be where we're at without you.

Andrew, you're a good person and someone I admire. Now you've been acknowledged in a book twice.

Norman Eng, your speech at lunch changed everything. I owe you one, big time. Twenty years later and I still dress better than you.

Lastly, to my beautiful wife, Lisa. I could not have written this book without your help and support.

Thank you all.

Table of Contents

Introduction

None of what I have written in this book exposes proprietary information or violates any non-disclosure agreements I've signed. All of my research was done with public information that is readily available from the Consumer Finance Protection Bureau, in print, online or included in marketing campaigns. When appropriate, I have cited my resource.

I began my mortgage career at Fremont Investment & Loan (also known as Fremont). Those of you old enough to know about Fremont–congratulations, you are officially a seasoned mortgage veteran. For those of you unfamiliar–Fremont was founded in 1937 as Investors Thrift & Loan. The company was acquired by Fremont General Corp. in 1990 and later renamed to "Fremont Investment & Loan."

The firm evolved into one of the country's largest subprime lenders, becoming a $7 billion financial services firm. It continued to be a major player until March of 2007.

Because I came to Fremont from a non-finance industry, specifically advertising and marketing, I was put into an in-depth training program to become a wholesale account executive (AE). The program was very thorough. As an example, we spent an entire month on the origins, terms, and principles of the modern mortgage. We learned things like the origin of the 30-year amortized mortgage. Banks originally gave balloon loans with three- to five-year terms? After the stock market crash of 1929 investors stopped buying mortgage bonds. It wasn't until 1934 that the Federal Housing Administration stepped in with a program to insure mortgages, an amortization plan, and loan terms of 15 to 20 years (PK).

Along with learning about the modern-day mortgage, we spent another two months reviewing Fremont's programs, work flow, and underwriting guidelines. After three months we went out into the field and were assigned a mentor. Our mentor helped us with the day-to-day challenges of being an AE, and occasionally we came back to the corporate office to see where our heads were at and what we needed help with. In total, the training program lasted six months. To this day, I consider the training I received at Fremont to be the industry gold standard.

Nowadays a new AE is lucky to get a three-day cram session on the products their lender offers.

With that, let's address the 800-pound gorilla in the room. It's hard not to make the comparison, but non-QM is not a revival of sub-prime lending. Subprime lenders of the past prioritized the equity of the subject property over the borrower's ability to pay back the loan. Does anyone remember the 80/20 stated loan? A Countrywide Financial executive famously said, "We will give a loan to anyone who can fog a mirror." For those of you who forgot, or don't know, Countrywide Financial was founded in 1968 by Angelo Mozilo and by 1992 was the largest originator of single-family mortgages in the country. In 2006 it ranked 122 on the Fortune 500, with $18.5 billion in revenue and $2.4 billion in pro ts, and generated $490 billion in loans. By August of 2007, Wall Street bankers cut off Countrywide's short-term funding, which debilitated its ability to operate. A few months later, Countrywide had to choose between bankruptcy or acquisition. In January 2008, Bank of America announced that it would buy Countrywide for $4 billion dollars—a fraction of what Countrywide was worth at its peak. Since then, new rules (imposed by Dodd-Frank and the Consumer Finance Protection Bureau) protect mortgage lenders from liability when originating qualified mortgage loans. This allows lenders to make home loans with less fear of lawsuits and financial loss. A non-QM loan is not inherently high-risk. It's a loan that doesn't conform to the complex and stringent rules of a Qualified Mortgage. In today's environment, you have to do a lot more than just fog a mirror to get a loan.

This book is an insider's guide to non-QM loans. It was written to show mortgage loan originators how to make more money but I'll let you in on a secret–there are a lot of good AEs that don't know half the things in this book. I'm not knocking them; like I said, companies are not willing to invest in their employees like Fremont did. If you know an AE that's struggling, tell them about this book. If you're an AE and you know you have holes in your game, read the book. Every day I field calls from AEs, mortgage brokers, and mortgage loan originators asking me to advise them. I help everyone without hesitation, and I do it with a smile.

Throughout the book I will be using terms and lingo I assume you know as a seasoned mortgage professional. As an example, when I say DTI, I assume you know that means Debt-to-Income Ratio. Furthermore, I assume you know DTI is expressed as a percentage and is your total minimum monthly debt divided by your gross monthly income. On occasion, when I feel a word or term is specific to non-QM, I'll define the word or term and explain its significance. As regulations change, product offering will change; in the process I hope to offer updated book editions. Regulations and guidelines are a dry subject matter. I can't make it sexy, but I'll do my best to make it interesting.

I don't consider myself to be an expert, and it is my opinion there are no experts. Let me explain. In the 1990s, the argument for sub-prime loans went something like this: Lenders, encouraged by a variety of government agencies, offered a two-year adjustable rate mortgage to borrowers who traditionally did not qualify for conventional loans. These borrowers may have had derogatory payments on credit cards, auto loans, or a recent life event such as a bankruptcy or foreclosure. A low starting rate on an ARM gave the borrower two years to clean up their credit and refinance into a conventional loan. In addition, conventional wisdom had it that homeownership fostered widespread economic benefits through job creation and other economic stimuli. As an example, the more people who owned homes, the more cans of paints would be needed, more trash cans sold, and more lawn mowers acquired in order to groom the lawns of all those new home owners. It all sounds good and in theory it makes sense.

There was one problem, however: What happens when home values drop, your interest rate adjusts upward, and you owe more than your house is worth?

That perfect storm is now referred to as the Great Recession and lasted from December 2007 to June 2009 (The Great Recession). How could all the prestigious academic banking executives and lawmakers be wrong? Several books have already been written on that subject.

I'd also like to point out that I'm not a lawyer. There are a lot of regulations, rules, sections, updates, guidelines, and other documents that complicate our lives. If you have legal questions about regulations then you need a compliance lawyer. In my experience, you can follow this rabbit hole as deep as you want to go and still not have a clear understanding of the industry. So, you may be asking yourself, what gives me the right to author a book about non-QM loans? I'm a guy with 15 years' experience as a non-prime AE. As of right now (at my company) I'm consistently in the upper 15 percent of submitted units, the upper 7 percent of overall units, and the upper 10 percent in bringing in new customers. However, now that the book is complete and I have some of my free time back, I plan on smashing all previously held records. In addition, I read the pertinent compliance guidelines put out by the CFPB and I've translated them from legalese into less technical English. I understand why lenders are confident in offering these loans. I understand guidelines and how they tie into the regulations. Lastly, I took and passed the federal mortgage licensing test and 12 individual state licensing tests in 14 days, smashing the previously held company record of 16 days. Unfortunately, it was a record no one really cared about except me. Think of me as a fishing guide. If you want a successful fishing trip, it's your guide's job to know the lake, stream or river and how to catch the fish within it. Do you really care about water temperature, mating habits, what flies are hatching, etc.? No, you just want to catch fish. If you have a loan that needs to fund do you really care about the repeal of the Gram-Leach-Bliley Act, mortgage securitization, or the implementation of the Wall Street Reform Act? No, you just want to fund your loan. This book will help you make more money by funding more non-QM loans.

Chapter One

The Future of Non-Qualified Mortgages

In December of 2017, the Federal Reserve showed continued optimism in the U.S. economy by voting to raise short-term interest rates for the third time that year–signaling that it would stay on a similar path in 2018. Through the nearly nine-year bull market run, the Federal Reserve held rates at or near zero; however, recent signs of rising inflation are pushing the central bank into hiking rates more aggressively–which can have far-reaching consequences for consumers. BlackRock's Chief Investment Officer, Rick Rieder, recently said, "Inflation is accelerating and may well push interest rates higher, allowing the

Federal Reserve to move policy rates three times this year [2018] perhaps even four."

As one of the Big 3 credit rating agencies (S&P, Moody's and Fitch Group), S&P Global Rating is a leading providers of corporate credit ratings. They're in 28 countries around the world and have a history that dates back more than 150 years. S&P Global Rating provides high-quality market intelligence in the form of credit ratings, research, and thought leadership. In December of 2017, S&P Global Rating expressed their confidence in the performance of non-qualified mortgages (non-QM) and stated they expect (Gaffney) the non-QM market to double–or even triple–in 2018. When releasing their forecast (Gaffney) they explained that, despite misrepresentation in the media, the non-QM loans of today are not simply a reincarnation of subprime products which proliferated before the great recession.

The Mortgage Bankers Association (MBA) is the United States national association representing all facets of the real estate finance industry (Wikipedia Contributors). Headquartered in Washington D.C., the MBA represents over 2,200 member companies. On October 24, 2017, the MBA announced that they expect to see $1.2 trillion in purchase mortgage originations during 2018; a 7.3 percent increase (Ahmad) from the year prior. In contrast, the MBA anticipates that refinance originations will decrease in 2018 by 28.3 percent from 2017 to approximately $430 billion (Ahmad). In total, mortgage originations (purchases and refinances) are anticipated to decrease by $90 billion in 2018 (Ahmad).

To summarize, rates are going up, originations are going down, and according to S&P Global rating, non-QM loans are expected to double or triple. If you are a mortgage broker (or a mortgage loan originator) and your income is getting progressively smaller, I want you to think about your business model for the next one to five years. Is your current plan applicable in today's environment or do you need to adapt? I'm sure you've heard the term, "Strike while the iron is hot." The term is in reference to striking a hot piece of metal while it's hot enough to be shaped. Today the term means to act on an opportunity promptly. The time to strike and shape your future is now!

Chapter Two

How Lenders are Able to Offer Non-Qualified Mortgage Loans

In an attempt to weaken British trade routes and exert influence, the French–spearheaded by General Napoleon Bonaparte–invaded Egypt in 1798 (Wikipedia Contributors). In the town of Rosetta, on the Mediterranean coast of Egypt, members of Napoleon's army dug for materials in order to make additions to a fort. There they found a stone inscribed with three different languages used in Egypt at the time: Ancient Egyptian (hieroglyphics), Demotic Script, and Ancient Greek. The stone was eventually deemed valuable and preserved. After the British's defeat of the French, the stone was handed over to British authorities along with other antiquities. It then went on to be studied in detail by several linguists from many different countries, and is now referred to as the Rosetta Stone. The Rosetta Stone is one of the most famous artifacts in all of archeology, as it was the key to unlocking the code of Egyptian Hieroglyphics—making the translation of the pictorial writing system possible (Thebritishmuseum.org).

Have you received an approval and thought to yourself, *Why in the world is the underwriter asking for this condition?* You immediately call your AE and say, "Why are they asking for this?"

"I don't know," responds your AE, promising to look into it. All the while you're pulling out your hair, the loan is being delayed, and the underwriter is being insistent. Wouldn't it be nice to have had a Rosetta Stone for the mortgage industry? A way to understand what the underwriter is thinking and translate it into English? Then you could know the thought process behind the condition, explain to the borrower why it's needed, or offer different documentation to get your loan closed. Well, I have good news for you: there is a Rosetta Stone for non-QM lending and it's called Ability-to-Repay (ATR).

In 2009, and in response to the 2008 financial crisis, the Board of Governors of the Federal Reserve System adopted a rule under the Truth-In-Lending Act. This rule prohibited lenders from making higher-priced mortgages without first assessing a consumer's ability to repay the loan. In 2010 the Dodd-Frank Wall Street Reform Act (also known as just the Dodd-Frank Act) also adopted similar ATR requirements for virtually all residential mortgage loans. At that time, Congress established a "presumption of compliance" with ATR requirements for a certain category of mortgages called qualified mortgages (QM). I'll dive deeper into "presumption of compliance" a bit down the road. Lastly, in January of 2013 the CFPB adopted a rule that implemented the ATR provision of the Dodd-Frank Act. In March of 2013 Citadel Servicing Corp. became the first lender to enter the Non-QM lending space. Now that lenders were aware of the rules of the game, many more lenders began joining the space.

1. HomeXpress Mortgage
2. Angel Oak
3. Lendsure Mortgage Corp.
4. Sprout Mortgage
5. Impac Mortgage

By no means is this a comprehensive list; however, these are some of the most notable.

So, what is ATR? The ATR rule requires a lender to make a reasonable good-faith determination before or when a mortgage loan is consummated that the borrower has a reasonable ability to repay. I'll say it again because it's important: The lender must make a reasonable good-faith determination that the borrower has the ability to repay the loan. Under ATR there are eight underwriting factors that must be considered to meet the requirements of the rule. Creditors can consider other factors but should show certain evidence that the eight specified factors have been addressed. Without going into great detail, the factors are:

1. Current or reasonably expected income or assets that the consumer will rely on to repay the loan.
2. Current employment status (if you rely on employment income when assessing the consumer's ability to repay).
3. Projected monthly mortgage payment for this loan.
4. Projected monthly payment on any simultaneous loans secured by the same property.
5. Monthly payments for property taxes and insurance that you require the consumer to buy, and certain other costs related to the property such as homeowner's association fees.
6. Debts, alimony, and child-support obligations.
7. Monthly debt-to-income ratio or residual income.
8. Credit history. Creditors must generally use reasonably reliable third-party records to verify the information they use to evaluate the factors.

ATR is the cornerstone of residential mortgage lending, and lenders are responsible for developing and applying their own underwriting standards as well as making changes (where applicable) to account for changes in regulations or economic fluctuations. I know I said I wouldn't delve into the minutiae, but this is important. ATR is the foundation of all the products offered in the non-QM space.

Now we know what ATR is–its history and importance in residential mortgage lending. The next step in this chain of logic is to show how it impacts non-QM loans and how they're originated. This can be explained in several different ways. There are some who may disagree with my interpretation of the various regulations; however, the basis of this book is to provide a simplified understanding of non-QM, and for that my explanation is appropriate.

Whether or not a lender complied with the ATR requirements is based on the information available during the origination. For example, a lender is not in violation of the ATR requirement if consumers can't repay their mortgage loan due to a sudden and unexpected loss of employment after the loan was originated. On the other hand, if a borrower is having trouble paying a loan they could claim that the lender failed to make a reasonable good-faith determination of their ATR. If the consumer proves this claim in court then the lender will be held liable. There are three distinct levels of liability when it comes to ATR: Presumption of Compliance and Safe Harbor, Rebuttable Presumption, and Non-QM.

Presumption of Compliance and Safe Harbor

The Dodd-Frank Act provides that qualified mortgages are entitled to a presumption that the lender making the loan satisfied the ability-to-repay requirements. For the layman, if you originate a loan that's not higher priced and go through all the hoops needed to fund a qualified mortgage, your loan is then given Safe Harbor status. Safe Harbor loans are conclusively presumed to comply with the ATR requirement. As such, it's very difficult to find a lender liable for failing to make a good-faith effort in determining a borrower's ATR if the loan has been given Safe Harbor status. This is your standard conventional loan.

Rebuttable Presumption

Mortgages with an annual percentage rate that exceeds the average prime offer rate by a specified percentage are referred to as "higher priced mortgages." I won't get into the math involved, because it's not important to us now. Qualified mortgages that are higher priced have Rebuttable Presumptions that comply with ATR requirements. In layman's terms, higher priced qualified mortgages are presumed to have complied with the ATR rule; however, the court is open to the claim the lender did not make a reasonable good-faith determination to ensure the borrower had an ability to repay. This is a tall order. The borrower must show, based on the information available at the time the mortgage was made, that they did not have enough income to meet living expenses, pay the mortgage, and repay other debts. In this day and age someone would have had to drop the ball, big time.

Non-Qualified Mortgages

Non-qualified mortgages are not offered any of the legal protections of qualified mortgages. Now that I've written the sentence it seems obvious; nonetheless, I felt it necessary to put it in writing. There is no presumption of compliance with the ATR rule, and there is no rebuttable presumption. If a borrower decides to file a suit against the lender, it is entirely incumbent upon the lender to show that they made a reasonable good-faith determination that the borrower had the ability to repay it. After I submit a loan, my clients receive the following email from me:

> Hello,
>
> Your loan has been submitted to our Set-Up department. The Intent to Proceed will be produced by the lender–along with other disclosures–shortly after the loan is successfully reviewed. Typically we'll receive an approval 2-3 days after the loan is submitted to underwriting. Please bear in mind that ACME Mortgage is a non-QM lender and does not underwrite to DU or LP, which are both automated underwriting systems used for qualified mortgages. We manually

underwrite all of our loans and we may require conditions not typical for conventional or government loans. If you have any questions, please feel free to call or email.

Sincerely,
Fernando Zoota

I've done a few things here. First, I've communicated with my customer, the mortgage broker, the successful submission of their loan. In turn, they can communicate this to their customer. Everyone is aware of the status of the loan and that's just being a good AE. Secondly, in mentioning the disclosures I let everyone know that the loan will be compliant with TRID. TRID is an acronym for Truth in Lending Act/Real Estate Settlement Procedures Act, Integrated Disclosure. Blah, that's a mouthful. Lastly, I set proper expectations that this is not a conventional loan or a qualified mortgage; this is a non-qualified mortgage. As such, we will ask for things that may not be typical in order to ensure we've made a reasonable good-faith determination. Don't get me wrong, non-QM loans are not harder to do. In many ways they're easier—especially if you understand Ability-to-Repay.

Our version of the Rosetta Stone is the Ability-to-Repay rule, which I outlined in this chapter. In it is everything we need know in order to translate the underwriter's conditions. If you get a condition that doesn't immediately make sense, ask yourself, "Of the eight factors used to determine a borrower's ability to repay, which one is addressed by this condition?" It may take a bit at first, but you'll get it. Once you've reviewed enough conditions in this context, you'll understand immediately. The faster you satisfy the conditions, the faster you will fund the loan and make money.

Chapter Three

What Non-Qualified Mortgage Products are Available?

In the early 1990s, boxing's heavyweight division was full of prospects all worthy of a shot at the title. After winning nine fights in a row (eight by knock-out and two hard fights with "Iron" Mike Tyson), many boxing fans considered Donovan "Razor" Ruddock as the world's best heavyweight. On October 31, 1992 he would meet Lennox Lewis, who had beaten the best Europe had to offer, as well as win gold in the 1988 Seoul Olympics. As the harder puncher, many experts predicted Ruddock to win, or at least to be Lewis's toughest test.

On the night of the event, Lewis fought the perfect fight. Followed by a missed jab from Ruddock, the first knockdown came after a big overhand right from Lewis at the end of the first round. With a big grin, Ruddock rose at the count of eight. Had the bell not rung to indicate the end of the round he might have been in big trouble. At the start of the second round Lewis attacked, landing with both rights and lefts. A left hook to the head bounced Ruddock into the ropes and onto the canvas for the second time. After standing up, a groggy Ruddock was decked again from a flurry of punches, prompting the referee to stop the fight. The quick ending was a surprise to most considering Ruddock fought twelve hard rounds with "Iron" Mike Tyson; however, it was no surprise to Lewis. "I realized, by watching [video] tape, [Ruddock] keeps his left hand really low," Lewis said of Ruddock. "Razor has never been in with a guy who throws a right hand as fast as me. I think I surprised him." (Kenny)

I've conveyed this story not to prepare you for your next big boxing match, but to instead impress upon you the importance of knowledge. Lewis had watched hours upon hours of videotape on Ruddock and was confident in his fight experience and knowledge as he stepped into the ring on October 31, 1992. As a mortgage loan originator your confidence is derived from knowing what non-QM programs are available for your borrowers. In this chapter,

I've laid out the most common products offered by non-QM lenders.

Non-QM lenders have a popular but limited product line. Most mortgage loan originators would admit that they don't know what they don't know about non-QM products. Conventional loans are commonly interchangeable with "conforming loans", since they are required to "conform" to Fannie Mae and Freddie Mac's underwriting requirements. An FHA loan is a mortgage issued by a federally qualified lender and insured by the Federal Housing Administration (FHA). The general thought is that if a loan is declined by a conventional or FHA lender, you should call a non-QM lender and see if they can do it. When identifying loans that can be funded by a non-QM lender, the jumping off point is to determine the purpose of the loan. The word "purpose" in the context of mortgage lending is determined by how the proceeds of the loan are to be used. There are a number of elements to consider, but it generally starts by identifying whether the loan is primarily for business or consumer purposes.

Consumer-Purpose Loans

The vast majority of loans originated in the non-QM lending space are consumer-purpose loans. This means that credit is offered or extended to a consumer primarily for personal, family, or household purposes. In addition, consumer-purpose loans are extended to people and not to entities like a trust or an LLC. Once a loan is determined to be for consumer purposes, the borrower is afforded certain rights under Regulation Z, which is part of the Truth in Lending Act of 1968 and was implemented to protect people when they use consumer credit. For example, the lender must comply with TRID. Just like a conventional loan, a loan estimate must be provided to the consumer–either in person or through the mail–no later than three business days following the receipt of an application.

Most non-QM loans fall into this bucket. The following are the most popular consumer-purpose programs currently available:

Bank Statements for Income: Hands down the bread and butter of the entire non-QM space is bank statements for income. In lieu of providing tax returns to document income, self-employed borrowers can provide either twelve or twenty-four months of business or personal bank statements. There's even a one-month bank statement program.

Asset Lending: This can be used in one of two ways. You can use liquid assets to either supplement documented income like pay stubs and W2's, or you can qualify for a loan entirely on the basis of a borrower's liquid assets.

Lease Agreements for Income: When refinancing a non-owner occupied property you can income-qualify by providing a lease agreement along with proof you're receiving the income (two months' canceled checks or banks statements showing the deposits).

Low FICO Scores: On average the lowest FICO score most conforming lenders will accept is 620. FICO is an abbreviation for the Fair Isaac Corporation, the first company to offer consumers a credit-risk model with a score. Scores range from 300 to 850. Non-QM lenders will accept scores as low as 500. On rare occasions, sub-500 scores can be reviewed on a case-by-case basis. The risk is offset by reduced loan to value, most commonly know as LTV and increased rates.

Recent Bankruptcies and/or Foreclosures: The waiting period for a borrower with a chapter 7 bankruptcy is four years for Fannie Mae & Freddie Mac. Without going into great detail, Fannie & Freddie are two government-sponsored enterprises whose purpose is to expand the secondary mortgage market by securitizing mortgages. The waiting period for FHA is two years–and the clock starts ticking after the discharge date. It's a little better for a chapter 13 bankruptcy. Foreclosures require a four-year seasoning period as well. In contrast, non-QM lenders require one day out of bankruptcy or foreclosure.

ITIN Borrowers: For those of you who don't know, ITIN stands for Individual Taxpayer Identification Number. The Internal Revenue Service (IRS), otherwise know as the nation's tax collection agency, created the ITIN for use by anyone who is not eligible to apply for a Social Security Number (SSN) but who receive taxable money. If you're in the United States with no legal status but are earning income, you can pay taxes with an ITIN. The number starts with a 9 and looks similar to an SSN. Not all non-QM lenders will lend to a borrower with an ITIN, so check with your AE.

Short-Term Rentals: A short term rental property is one that forgoes a long term lease and instead is rented multiple times a year for time periods less than 30 days. Companies like AirBnB or Vacation Rentals by Owner (VRBO) allow owners to list properties. If you're purchasing a short-term rental this doesn't apply; however, if you're refinancing and need to offset the property expense, you can provide a rental history from either AirBnB or VRBO to show the property's cash flow.

I've listed the most common and/or popular products offered by non-QM lenders. With that said, there may be additional loan programs available that I'm not familiar with.

Business-Purpose Loans

Regulation Z has two exemptions under which a loan would be considered business-purpose: first, loans to non-natural persons (usually this means loans to companies and not people); second, loans primarily for business or commercial purposes. In the non-QM world this primarily means purchasing or refinancing one- to four-unit rental properties. Because of this, a special rule exists for non-owner occupied rental properties. This means a loan to acquire, improve, or maintain a non-owner occupied rental property will always be deemed to be for business purposes. The following are the two most popular business-purpose loan programs:

Debt Service Coverage Ratio (DSCR): A lot of people refer to this as a stated loan or a loan where the lender does not verify the borrower's income. Don't call it "stated." If the subject property is non-owner occupied, DSCR allows you to qualify by using the lease agreement and/or a rent survey. Take the lease payment, or potential lease payment, and subtract the operating costs. This includes principal, interest, taxes, insurance, etc. The difference is the property's cash flow. In most cases, the property just has to have positive cash flow in order to qualify. In certain circumstances you can qualify with a negative cash flow.

It's important to note that these programs are primarily for buying and holding an investment property. This is not a loan program for fixing up a home and flipping it for a quick profit. Most lenders rely on the borrower holding the loan for at least a year in order for it to be profitable. Fix-and-flips are a loss for the lender, hence an undesirable loan product to offer.

Foreign Nationals: In the lending world, the definition of a foreign national is someone who lives and works abroad. They visit the United States occasionally for either business or pleasure. They can purchase a second home or an investment property, but never a primary residence. I like these loans a lot because they're simple. You're not evaluating income because it's earned overseas, and you're not reviewing credit because they don't have an SSN. The flip side is that the downpayment will most likely be 25 to 30 percent, and the interest rate will be high. I don't know if this is precisely a business-purpose loan; however, I do know the loan is not subject to Regulation Z or TRID.

These are not the only business-purpose loans offered, but they are the most popular. Like Lennox Lewis, confidence comes from your experience and knowledge as a mortgage loan originator. Know what products can be offered to your borrower, and quickly identify loans you can get funded. This kind of preparation will certainly get you the knock-out!

Chapter Four

Non-Qualified Mortgage Loans are Not . . .

In 1576, Martin Frobisher was the first English explorer to search for the Northwest Passage–the seaway linking the Atlantic and the Pacific Ocean. It took Frobisher five years to raise the funds. He eventually convinced an English merchant who was keen on discovering the Northwest Passage for trade purposes to fund the exploration. He made three failed attempts and only reached Canada's Northeast. After his first attempt, not wanting to return to England empty-handed, Frobisher brought back a small black stone thought to contain gold. The potential discovery of gold was enough for Frobisher's backers to fund additional voyages. On his second voyage, Frobisher returned to England with 200 tons of ore—which turned out to be worthless. Undeterred, a small armada of ships sailed a year later and returned with over 1,000 tons of ore. Uniquely built furnaces revealed that Frobisher's fleet had brought back nothing more than pyrite, more commonly know as "fool's gold."

On average, I review five loan scenarios a day. If you do the math, five loans a day times five days a week (with four weeks in a month) makes 100 loans a month. If an average loan is $250,000, that's a loan volume of $25 million a month. If only half the loans fund, that's still $12.5 million.

I know what you're thinking: I must be rich.

Well, I have bad news (for me): I'm not rich—not even close. You see, if I review 25 loans a week, more than half will be loans I can't do (i.e., fool's gold). While it's important to identify good loans, it's equally as important to identify the loans you can't do. The following is a list of the most common types of loans thought to be non-QM but in reality are not:

Hard Money: A large portion of non-QM loans are for the purchase or refinance of investment properties. This leads brokers to believe non-QM loans are synonymous with hard money loans. Hard money loans are primarily used to purchase a home, fix it up, and then quickly sell it for a handsome profit. Hard money loans are typically private investors where interest rates are much higher than conventional residential loans. Contrarily, in order for a non-QM loan to be profitable, a borrower must keep it for at least one year. While a fair amount of non-QM loans are investment properties, they are almost always bought and held, not fixed and flipped.

Conventional or Government: Non-QM loans are neither conventional nor government-sponsored. That is to say, the loans will not be sold to either Fannie Mae or Freddie Mac, and are not insured by a government agency like the Federal Housing Administration (FHA) or the Veterans Affairs (VA). Instead, non-QM loans are typically originated, held, and then later securitized as a mortgage-backed security. The reason it's important to quickly differentiate non-QM from conventional or government-sponsored loans is that a broker may have expectations of lower rates and higher LTV. On the flip side, many mortgage brokers and loan officers believe that their borrower will require mortgage insurance with an LTV above 80 percent, which is not true for non-QM loans.

Commercial: As I mentioned, a large portion of non-QM loans are for investment properties. This is typically a single-family residence, but also includes two- to four-unit properties. If a broker or a mortgage loan originator is unsure where to place a loan, who do they call? A non-QM lender. In this circumstance I usually refer the originator to a reputable commercial lender.

FHA 203K: For those of you unfamiliar: FHA 203k loans allow an applicant to borrow money for both home improvement and a home purchase using only one loan. Presently this type of loan does not exist in the non-QM space. I typically run into this with a borrower whom I've already prequalified for a loan to purchase a home. After, the mortgage loan originator will tell me the borrower has found a great deal on a home that's in need of repairs. "In need of repair" really means the home is uninhabitable. Now I'm being asked to finance the purchase of the home and the repairs needed to make the home suitable to live in. Non-QM lenders are only willing to lend on properties that are move-in ready. It's best to tell all parties involved as quickly as possible. This ensures we're focusing our energy on a property we can get approved.

Had Frobisher been able to determine his black rock contained pyrite and not gold, he would have saved himself a lot of time–and his investors a lot of money. It's important to identify good loans, but it's equally as important to identify loans that are not a fit. In this chapter we learned about the most common scenario you'll run across that can waste your time and energy or can lead to riches if properly thought through. If time is money (and, as we all know, it is), then this skill is most certainly a moneymaker.

Chapter Five

Choose The Best Lender and Account Executive

The Matrix is a 1999 science-fiction action film starring Keanu Reeves. It depicts a dystopian future in which reality, as perceived by most humans, is actually a simulated reality called the "Matrix." The Matrix is created by sentient machines to subdue the human population. Computer programmer Thomas Anderson (Mr. Anderson) lives a double life under the hacker alias, Neo. He believes something is wrong with the world and goes in search of a man named Morpheus–a man the government considers a terrorist. Neo meets Morpheus and is offered a choice–a red pill that will allow him to learn the truth about the

Matrix, or a blue pill that will return him to his former life. After he swallows the red pill, Neo's dystopian reality disintegrates and he's made aware of the truth for the very first time.

In your everyday reality as a mortgage loan originator, you will be presented with choices. Do I submit this loan to lender A or lender B? Like *The Matrix*, both choices will seem real, but danger is always lurking. Choose wisely and your experience will be positive; choose incorrectly and your world will be turned upside down. Great mortgage loan originators associate themselves with great lenders and have the sense enough to listen to their AE's guidance.

In this chapter I'll give you the knowledge to identify the best lenders to work with and why. In addition, once you've identified the right lender for you and your borrower, you'll need to identify the best available AE within that organization. I always say that a good AE can get a loan through a bad lender.

Types of Lenders

The residential mortgage industry is vast and complex. There seem to be an infinite number of institutions involved with an equally infinite number of ways to make or lose money; however, this book is about making money with non-QM loans. Within non-QM there are essentially two types of wholesale lenders: captive funds and conduit lenders. They both have their pros and cons depending on your needs as well as those of your borrower. It's important to identify which type of lender you will be working with.

Captive Funds Lender

A captive funds lender is a lender with a warehouse line of credit. A warehouse line of credit is provided to a mortgage lender to fund mortgages until the lender sells them in the secondary market. A warehouse line of credit comes in many different shapes and sizes depending on a company's years in business, origination volume, the corporate net worth, and many additional requirements. In order to purchase a home, a borrower–let's say Mr. Smith–gets a loan from a mortgage broker, American Mortgage Corp., in the amount of $250,000. American Mortgage Corp. brokers the loan to a non-QM wholesale lender named Fairmont Wholesale. Fairmont approves and funds the loan, but Fairmont does not lend him its own money–it instead borrows the money from a warehouse lender. One month later, Fairmont sells the mortgage to another lender and receives cash that it uses to repay the warehouse lender. American Mortgage Corp. profits by earning points, origination, underwriting and processing fees, as well as servicing rights (if applicable).

It's important to know if your lender has a warehouse line of credit so you are aware of the ground rules. Before a captive funds lender ever funds a single loan, they've identified who they will sell their loans to in the secondary market. It's probably more than one institution, and the strategy may vary depending on the loan products being offered. Because they've predetermined where they intend to sell their loans, they develop a set of guidelines that must be adhered to in order to recoup their capital investment. Ultimately, they want to sell all their loans. That being said, it is still their money and so they have the final say in approving a borrower's loan. In lending, time tends to be an issue; the longer a loan sits, the more likely it is to not get funded. Captive funds lenders tend to be the quicker of the two options available in non-QM.

Conduit Lender

The term "conduit lender" is used in several different ways in the lending industry, all with subtle differences. For the purpose of this book I will be using the term to describe a wholesale lender that does not have a warehouse line of credit. As discussed earlier, a warehouse line of credit is a big responsibility, requiring a substantial net worth and almost always requiring a personal guaranty. A conduit lender acts as, well, a conduit between the broker and the money. A conduit lender establishes the operation, which includes account executives, account managers, and underwriters; however, at the end of the process the money to fund the loans comes from another financial institution. The benefit for a broker in using a conduit lender can be lower rates or a niche product not offered by other non-QM lenders.

The downside is that loans tend to take longer to originate. The loan is underwritten not only by the wholesaler but also by the financial institution providing the money. I'm sure you've heard of or experienced a situation where a loan was ready to fund only to have a whole bunch of conditions piled onto the approval. Most likely that's the underwriter from the other financial institution reviewing the loan.

I'm not playing favorites; both types of wholesale lenders have their place. If you have a purchase, and time is an issue, you may want to submit your loan to a captive funds lender. If you have a refinance with no time constraints, it may be beneficial to submit your loan to a conduit lender with great rates. The key is knowing who you're working with. In either instance, after a loan is originated it will most likely be sold to a mortgage aggregator in order to free up capital to lower the lender's long-term risk.

Management

I'd like to take a brief moment to discuss the importance of executive management. As a mortgage broker, you may not have the luxury to pick and choose lenders based on management style. I'd like to point out the importance of researching the management team because their character can determine the success of your relationship with said lender.

It's been my experience that the personalities and management styles tend to trickle down from the executive staff through to the middle management, and ultimately saturate into the rank and file. A cruel dictatorial leader will tend to produce cruel managers, who in turn will treat their employees with cruelty. By the time you get on the phone with a representative, you're talking to a whipped dog who has little motivation to work on your file.

Conversely, considerate and generous leaders typically have no tolerance for rude or unprofessional behavior. As a result, the staff tends to reflect the values of the leadership team. While things will never go perfectly, you do get the sense people are working hard on your behalf.

In turn, don't be a jerk to your AE or the lender's staff. This is a small industry, and people decide quickly who they like to work with. Succesful AEs won't work with jerks, so if you're a jerk then only the desperate will work with you–and that won't be a pleasant experience. Some food for thought.

Choosing an Account Executive

The single most important thing you can do to ensure the success of your loan–and your business for that matter–is work with the best AE available to a specific lender. Not all loans will fund–that's a fact. In my experience, most borrowers are honest folks and genuine in their communications, but they say and do things that run contrary to closing a loan.

Mortgage Loan Originator: "Mr. Borrower, you said Mary Beth was your ex-wife, but the lenders say you're still legally married to her."

Mr. Borrower: "Well, she *is* my ex-wife. She just never saw fit to sign the paperwork to make it official."

Mortgage Loan Originator: "Okay. Now, if Mary Beth is your wife, who is Suzie Q?"

Mr. Borrower: "Suzie Q is my new wife. We have three beautiful kids together. We were never able to make it official because Mary Beth won't sign the paperwork!"

You see where this is going? I'm sure you've had similar situations. Borrowers can make things hard and it's your job as a loan originator to find the best solution for your borrower. It's impossible for a mortgage loan originator to know every single loan program available; a great AE will not only know the products he has available, but many of the products offered by his competitors. My customers view me as the expert, and because of that I always get the first phone call.

How do you choose the best available AE? If you noticed, I didn't say the best AE–I said the best *available*. Every lender has the best AE. I don't mean the most successful–I mean the best. This means the nicest, most knowledgeable, and most readily accessible. The rub is that the best AEs are the busiest and often don't accept new brokers unless it a high producing office. In that instance, your job is to locate the best available AE. You have to recognize that there are two types of AEs within a lender. I don't mean junior account executive, senior account executive, or even national account executive. I mean, there are two types of sales positions within a lender, the account executives and the producing managers. I don't like this structure, but it's just how it is. What's the difference?

Account Executive: In plain English–the job of an AE is to assist the mortgage loan originator to identify a potential borrower, assemble a loan submission package, navigate the loan through underwriting, help clear conditions, and in general make sure their loan funds. In return, they are paid a commission–primarily on loan volume (or amount).

Producing Manager: It is my experience that lenders offer successful AEs a sales manager position; however, the employees soon learn that there is more money to be made as an AE than as a manager. A producing manager has the same exact role as an AE with the added responsibility of managing a sales team. This includes responding to questions, distributing leads, producing reports, and so on. It's important to understand that most compensation plans unintentionally encourage a producing manager to focus on funding loans as opposed to building a sales team. As a manager within the organization, they're also held in higher regard with the other managers within the operations department. Does that help them get more loans closed? Maybe. A producing manager is also in the envious position of distributing accounts and leads. As a manager, it takes a special individual to hand over a million-dollar lead to a subordinate when they rely on funding to make most of their income.

When interviewing an AE, make sure to ask real questions. How long have they been a non-QM AE? If he's brand new, this may not be the right guy for you. Non-QM is totally different than conventional lending, and you need an expert. If he was an AE twelve years ago for New Century Mortgage Corporation and this is his first job back as an AE, then this may not be your guy. As you've noticed, non-QM is not subprime. There are a lot of new regulations that will make your head spin off of your shoulders. Are they a producing manager or an account executive? There's no right or wrong answer, but you need to know.

Also, what area does he serve? There are two philosophies: soliciting loans from every state, or focusing on a specific region. Some AEs cast their net wide and far, soliciting loans from every state in the Union. On the other hand, I prefer to focus on a specific region. I almost exclusively focus on the great state of Texas, but consider my territory to be the Southwest. Because of this, I am an expert in a specific territory. I know the laws and regulations inside and out. That's not to say I don't accept loans outside of my region, but in general I want my customers to consider me an expert–that means always having an answer.

I'm reminded of a story (Feingold) about an American tourist who was attacked by a lion in South Africa. Driving in a vehicle–and against her guide's strict instructions–the tourist rolled down the passenger window in order to photograph a group of lions. Apparently, she didn't notice that one of the lions was approaching from the side. The animal then lunged at the car, biting the woman through the open window. While trying to fend off the lion, the guide suffered a heart attack along with deep bites and cuts.

Originating loans is not nearly as exciting as an African safari, nor is it as dangerous. You also don't put your life in the hands of a trusted guide; however, you do put your livelihood in the hands of a trusted AE. After you've painstakingly invested your valuable time and effort in choosing an AE–for goodness sake, please listen to them! If they give you specific instructions, follow them. If they have taken their time to craft an email, read it. I can't tell you how many times I've written emails, and given instructions, only to be ignored. "Send this, don't send that." A good AE is your guide to funding a loan. When you make money, they make money, and the best way to make money is to follow instructions.

In order to make money, you need to work with the best lenders and AEs.

In this chapter, you learned the skills necessary to choose the best of both worlds. Do you work with a captive funds lender or a conduit lender? Are you working with an AE or a producing manager? There is no silver bullet–just best choices for your situation. A red pill or a blue pill as it were.

Chapter Six

Non-Qualified Mortgage Guidelines

Long ago, and against the wishes of my girlfriend (now my wife), I bought a Porsche 911. One day, driving at an unknown speed well above the posted speed limit, I saw the flashing lights of the highway patrol. I pulled over, rolled down my window, and handed my license and registration over to the officer. "Do you know why I pulled you over?" I never assume, so I answered, "No sir, I don't." He continued, "I clocked you speeding. Do you know how fast you were going!" In all sincerity, I didn't know how fast I was going. Again, I claimed ignorance. "No sir, I don't know how fast I was going." He continued again,

"Well, I clocked you going 95 miles an hour." Crap, I thought, that's fast. Then I remember something I read many years ago. "Sir, with all do respect, can I review the time stamp on the radar gun?" He responded, "Um, well . . . Let's see here. Well, I'll be! I didn't actually clock you speeding. Seems your car is too low to the ground." Huh, I thought, this is an interesting turn of events.

The Highway patrol officer asked me to admit to speeding and sign the ticket. If I didn't, he would state on the ticket I was speeding well over 100 miles per hour. The penalties for speeding over 100 miles per hour are grave. I didn't agree to speeding and asked the officer to note on the ticket that he was unable to clock my speed. Prior to court, I subpoenaed the officer's notes. Right there, in black and white, the officer noted that I would most likely fight the ticket and win. He never showed up to court. I did everything right completely by accident. The officer asserted I was speeding, but I never admitted to speeding and it was incumbent upon the officer to provide proof–of which he had none.

When pulling me over for speeding, both the officer and I were governed by the rule of law. In the lending industry, all parties involved are governed by the guidelines which are fashioned after compliance rules and regulations. In this chapter I'll share with you the most common guideline questions and how they vary from conventional loans. With this information you'll be sure to "beat the ticket."

Programs

At the time this book was written, all non-QM lenders divide their loan products into three buckets. In order of importance they are non-prime, investor loan products, and alt-A. The names will vary, but essentially the buckets will be consistent.

Non-Prime: Non-prime is a standard term used by most lenders to describe loans that fall outside conventional lending standards. In general, this bucket accounts for 85 percent of non-QM lending.

Investor Loan Products: This group of loans primarily consists of business purpose loans. The most common example is the purchase or refinances of an investment property qualifying under a debt services coverage ratio. This tends to be the second most popular reason to use a non-QM lender.

Alt-A: Alt-A is an alternative to conventional or A paper loan. An Alt-A borrower shares many of the characteristics of a prime borrower with one or more exceptions. The exceptions will vary, but a common example would be a recent life event such as a bankruptcy or foreclosure. In my experience, non-QM lenders don't get the first call for these types of loans and this bucket tends to be the least used.

Property Types

Non-QM loans benefit good borrowers who do not fulfill the requirements of strict conventional guidelines. The same can not be said for collateral that does not fulfill the requirement of conventional guidelines. Built into the business model is an acceptance of increased risk. There is no appetite for additional levels of risk by accepting unusual property types as collateral. Keep it standard and stay away from log homes and geodesic domes. Below is a standard list of properties non-QM lenders find acceptable. Keep in mind that all lenders are different and some lenders may choose not to lend on property types included on the list.

Single Family Residence: This is your standard, stick-built lot on a block. That is to say it's a traditionally built, free-standing residential home accepted by all lenders.

Two- to Four-Units: This type of property has two to four separate housing units for residential inhabitants within one building or several buildings on a given property. More than four units would make the property commercial, which would require a commercial lender.

Condominium: A condominium is one of a group of housing units where each homeowner owns their individual unit space, and all the dwellings share ownership of common use areas. This can be in either a low or high-rise structure.

Non-Warrantable Condominium: A condominium is deemed non-warrantable when it does not meet criteria set forth by Fannie Mae and Freddie Mac to allow for mortgage financing. Lenders are most willing to lend if a condo has obtained its non-warrantable status due to the percentage of non-owner-occupied units exceeding 50 percent of total units.

Condotel: The definition of "condotel" is a condominium project that is operated as a hotel with a registration desk, cleaning service, and more. The units are individually owned and unit owners also have the option to place their unit in the hotel's rental program where it is rented out like any other hotel room.

Acreage: Most non-QM lenders will consider lending on a home situated on up to five acres. A property with greater than five acres runs the risk of being considered rural. A rural property will have limited LTV and loan size. Use the Starbucks test to determine if a property is rural. Plug the address into Google Maps and if the closest Starbucks is greater than two miles away then the property is rural.

Property Value

As with any lender, an appraisal will be required to determine the value of a property being used as collateral for a loan. Most non-QM lenders are relatively small compared to conventional lenders. Because of this, assessing value is handled differently, but is still in compliance.

Uniform Residential Appraisal Report: Appraisals are typically ordered by the mortgage broker from an appraisal management company (AMC). An AMC is an independent entity through which mortgage professionals order residential appraisals (Form 1004). AMCs fulfill an administrative function in the appraisal process, including selecting an appraiser and delivering an appraisal report to the lender. Individual appraisers who work for AMCs provide the actual property valuation service.

Broker Price Opinion (BPO): A BPO is the estimated value of a property determined by a real estate broker, other qualified individual, or firm. A BPO is never used in lieu of an appraisal, but as a supplement to the appraisal. In addition, a BPO is not given more weight than an appraisal. If a BPO comes in with a lower value, comparables used in the BPO will need to be addressed by the appraiser in an appraisal addendum. In my experience, the appraiser is the defacto expert and tends to override the BPO if the comparables have been addressed properly.

Debt Services Coverage Ratio (DSCR)

DSCR loans are relatively simple to do and I enjoy getting them because there is less to do. As a reminder, DSCR loans are for purchasing or refinancing investment properties where you're using the property's cash-flow to income qualify. You have to credit quality, but in general you just have to make sure you're taking in more money than the home will cost you.

Comparable Rent Schedule: In either a refinance or a purchase you'll be required to order a comparable rent Sschedule along with your appraisal. For a single-family residence, it's Form 1007 or for two- to four-unit properties, it's Form 1025 that will be required to fulfill this condition. In a purchase the forms are used to determine your property's cash-flow. In a refinance they're used to make sure your lease is in alignment with the market.

Lease Agreements: A lease agreement will be required when refinancing an investment property to determine cash-flow. Along with the lease, you will most likely be required to provide the two most recent canceled rent checks to make sure you're actually receiving the rent. Your lease agreement will be compared to the comparable rent schedule ordered along with the appraisal.

Appraised Value: The most common reason for refinancing an investment property is to get out of a hard-money loan. A hard-money loan is a short-term, high-interest-rate loan typically offered by private investors. Hard-money is often used to purchase a home, fix it up, and sell it for a profit. When the time is running out on the terms of the loan, and extremely high penalties start bearing down on a borrower, they become motivated to refinance out of the hard-money loan and into more permanent financing. A non-QM lender is an ideal candidate for a refinance since they typically only require six months to have lapsed since the purchase of the home in order to use the new appraised value for purposes of LTV. Borrowers always want to use the new appraised value because it should be much greater than the recent purchase price.

Taxes & Insurance

You will get this question a lot and the answer is always the same. Regulation Z currently requires creditors to establish escrow accounts for higher-priced mortgage loans secured by a first lien on a principal dwelling. This practice has been adopted for all loans funded by non-QM lenders.

Bankruptcies

Recently, Fannie Mae changed its mortgage rules for borrowers with a recent chapter 7 bankruptcy. The group has reduced its mandatory waiting period after such an event from four down to two years. The change nearly mirrors a similar update from the FHA. In contrast, to qualify for a non-QM loan with limited LTV, a borrower simply has to have completed his bankruptcy and have at least one-day seasoning. Below is a list of the most common types of bankruptcies.

Chapter 7: A chapter 7 bankruptcy allows individuals to liquidate assets and distribute funds received through liquidation to creditors. Seasoning for a chapter 7 bankruptcy is calculatd using the discharge date reflected in the credit report or within the bankruptcy's discharge papers. Chapter 7 bankruptcies must be discharged prior to the loan application.

Chapter 13: Chapter 13 permits the debtor to file a plan to pay a certain percentage of future income to the bankruptcy court for payment to creditors. If the court approves the plan, the debtor will be under the court's protection while repaying stated debts. The chapter 13 filing date is used for seasoning for qualification purposes. The payment history should verify that all payments under the plan have been completed. FHA rules allow a lender to consider approving an FHA loan application from a borrower who is still paying on a chapter 13 bankruptcy. Unlike FHA, non-QM lenders require any open chapter 13 bankruptcies to be paid in full prior to or through closing.

Chapter 11: A chapter 11 bankruptcy is not as common as a chapter 7 or a chapter 13, but still worth mentioning. Chapter 11 allows businesses the opportunity to reorganize business debt obligations without having to liquidate all assets. Similar to a chapter 13, the debtor introduces a plan to creditors, which will allow the debtor to reorganize financial obligations to improve the financial stability of the business. Chapter 11 bankruptcies must be discharged prior to the loan application.

Foreclosures

Traditionally, FHA loans are the most forgiving of foreclosures. To qualify for an FHA mortgage loan you must wait at least three years after the foreclosure. There's an additional sticking point if the foreclosure involved an FHA loan. Prior to June 20, 2010, the waiting period for a Fannie Mae or Freddie Mac loan required waiting at least seven years after the foreclosure. Similar to a bankruptcy, to qualify for a non-QM loan, with limited LTV, a borrower simply has to have completed the foreclosure process. It's important to note, for seasoning purposes, the clock starts ticking from the time that foreclosure case has ended–which is the date that the prior home was sold in the foreclosure proceedings.

Depth of Credit

The standard rule regarding the depth of credit is three trade lines, rated for twenty-four months or more, and in good standing. There's typically some flexibility if the borrower does not have three open trade lines rated for twenty-four months. It may be acceptable if the borrower has an old closed account that was in good standing and rated for twenty-four months, and if combined with current open tradelines. The depth of credit usually becomes an issue only with people new to the country and here on a VISA. With limited LTV, many lenders will make accommodations in these situations.

Student Loans

I recently read that the Federal Government is well on its way towards lending more money in student loans than are repaid. The rising cost of the federal student loan program is due, in large part, to the growing number of borrowers enrolling in income-driven repayment programs, which allow them to repay their loans for a set period of time in correlation to how much money they make.

Non-QM lenders require payments on student loans to be included in the debt to income ratio regardless of deferment status. A one percent minimum payment will be used for qualification on all studen loans where a payment is not specified on the credit report.

Prepayment Penalty

On January 10, 2014, new rules were put forth by the Consumer Financial Protection Bureau (CFPB) prohibiting prepayment penalties for most residential mortgage loans, except under a few specific circumstances. Under the new rules, a prepayment penalty is allowed only if all the following are true:

1. The loan's APR cannot increase after you take out the loan (fixed rate)
2. The loan is a qualified mortgage
3. The loan is not a higher-priced mortgage

Does this sound like a non-QM loan? No. In fact, it sounds like the exact opposite. At this point in time, because of the CFPB's rules, most non-QM loans do not have a prepayment penalty. However, because business purpose loans are not regulated by the Dodd-Frank Act, Wall Street Reform Act, or DSCR many of the loans for an investment property may be subject to a prepayment penalty.

Fraud Risk Protection

One of the things I really enjoy about my job is picking and choosing who I wish to work with. My desire to work with someone usually comes down to two things: competency and honesty. I like to work with people who know what they're doing or who have a willingness to learn. Non-QM is relatively new to the market so I expect a learning curve. The other thing I'm insistent upon is honesty. For the most part, the liars and cheaters have been drummed out of the industry. On occasion, I hear a scenario that just doesn't smell right and my intuition is usually correct. Most of the time it's not a dishonest mortgage broker, but an uneducated borrower. "She's my ex-wife, but we haven't gotten a divorce," "I plan on moving in, but I don't know when," or "I didn't mention it because I didn't think it was important." With modern technology it's important for all parties to be aware that lenders now utilize fraud risk protection services. This is a service, provided by a third party vendor, that helps to detect fraud in mortgage applications, maintains compliance with regulations, and improves the application review process by offering greater speed, efficiency, and increased loan quality. Essentially, lenders pull a complete and detailed report on all parties involved in the loan process. If you or your borrower is hiding something we will find out!

When I got pulled over by the highway patrol I was lucky. I said and did everything correctly, and because of that the ticket was invalidated. When structuring a non-QM loan for underwriting, you don't need to be lucky. In previous chapters I explained the rules and regulations that shape underwriting guidelines. In this chapter I've given you a sneak-peek at the most common underwriting questions and how non-QM guidelines differ from conventional loan guidelines. Keep both hands on the wheel, don't exceed the posted speed limited, and always stay within the guidelines.

Chapter Seven

Submitting a Non-Qualified Mortgage Loan

According to the latest industry research, about 90 percent of the drugs that reach clinical trials never make it to FDA approval. Initially, one could conclude that a stringent FDA review process ensures only products with a clinical benefit safely reach the consumer; however, a more detailed analysis of clinical research programs tell a different story. Half of all drug development programs are rejected for reasons unrelated to the drug itself. These setbacks include inadequately maintained protocols (guidelines agreed to in advance), failure to follow the FDA's feedback, and delayed response to FDA inquiries.

With just one day's delay, millions of dollars in revenue are lost simply because required forms were filled out late, improperly, or responses to questions are replied to incorrectly.

Unlike the manufacturing of drugs, as a mortgage professional, we don't run the risk of losing millions of dollars over one deal; however, you can lose money for yourself–and worse–your borrower. Conventional loans are the easiest to originate. You run either Desktop Underwriter (DU) or Loan Prospector (LP) software, and the findings instruct you how to proceed. Follow the instructions, provide the documents, and–as long as nothing seems suspicious–you're good to go. Non-QM is a little more complicated, but if done properly it's not difficult. This chapter will educate you on how to properly submit a loan to your lender and prevent you from making common mistakes that can cost you money.

Submission Documents

As a reminder, non-QM lenders do not sell to Fannie, Freddie, or any other government sponsored entities. Because of this, we do not underwrite to DU or LP. Non-QM lenders manually underwrite loans which makes our process different than most lenders. Below is a list of standard items needed for a submission. Due to technical limitations, non-QM lenders generally do not have a portal to submit loans. This will be discussed later and in more detail.

Submission Forms: All lenders will have lender specific submission forms. It's important that you complete the forms in their entirety, because the forms give you (as the broker) an opportunity to tell your story. For example: are all the parties involved, what program did you discuss with your AE, confirmation of the loan amount, LTV, CLTV, and DTI? Do you want a 30-year fixed loan or are you okay with an ARM? There are usually borrower's authorizations or documents lawyers think are important. Darn lawyers! For organizational purposes I always include the lender's specific forms into one PDF.

Form 1003 & Credit: I always speak of the 1003 and credit report in the same breath. Assuming the information is accurate when reviewed together, you get a complete picture of what you and your borrower are trying to accomplish. This goes without saying, but I feel I have to mention that the 1003 application must be accurate and complete. I recently reviewed a 1003 and credit. Based on the information within the document, I quoted a rate. When the disclosures were sent to the borrower, the rate was higher. I was anxious and thought I made a mistake, but upon further review, the information in the 1003 application was inaccurate. The loan amount on the 1003 application was higher than the purchase contract. Because of this, the loan amount fell below a tier which caused an increase to the rate. To maintain TRID compliance, lender's policies will differ depending on interpretation of the regulations. Ask your AE about dates and signatures on required forms.

It's also important to keep in mind that non-QM lenders require a broker to provide their own credit report; however, the lender will also pull a credit report. If you're holding your borrower's FICO score together with bubble gum and duct tape, you may have problems.

Income: For non-QM, income does not mean tax returns. The whole non-QM industry almost entirely exists to avoid providing tax returns. That doesn't mean it doesn't happen, but it isn't common. The bread and butter of non-QM lending are bank statements for income. This means you can provide up to twenty-four months of bank statements in lieu of tax returns. Providing twenty-four months of bank statements is the most popular program. For W2 wage earners, you can provide the two most recent pay stubs (assuming this accounts for the most recent thirty days and the past two years W2's). It's also not uncommon to use a combination of incomes depending on the circumstances.

Purchase Contract: If you're purchasing a home, obviously we will need a copy of the executed purchase contract. Make sure the names on the contract match up to the names on the loan application. I know this seems obvious, but it sometimes happens that the names differ.

Lease Agreement: If you're refinancing a rental property, be sure to provide the lease agreement and the two most recent canceled rent checks. If the property is vacant, be sure to ask your AE if that's allowed by their lender.

Title Insurance: Most commonly know as title, it is a policy to protect against unknown liens and levies against property, guaranteeing free and clear ownership of the home. Most lenders require title at the time of submission. For a refinancing this is critical, but for a purchase it is less important. When non-QM was first introduced to the market there was a contingent of brokers who submitted all their conventional loan fallout to non-QM lenders without first determining if the loan was a fit. This clogged the pipeline with unqualified loans or approved loans with unsatisfactory terms and conditions. Lenders spent a lot of money underwriting loans that would never fund. By requiring title at the time of submission it forced the broker's involvement, ensuring the submission of a complete and well thought-out loan (theoretically).

Fannie Mae Data File: Most, if not all non-QM lenders will require you to provide a Fannie Mae data file. The Fannie Mae file format is used in the mortgage industry and can be exported from a broker's loan origination system (LOS), such as Calyx Point or Encompass. By providing the file to the lender they're able to quickly and easily import the information into their LOS.

Disclosures

In order to stay compliant with the Truth-in Lending/RESPA Integrated Disclosure rule (TRID), do not collect any fees for an appraisal or BPO until the lender's intent to proceed has been acknowledged by the borrower(s) after receipt of the loan estimate (LE). Typically, the intent to proceed is produced by the lender, along with other disclosures, shortly after the loan has been submitted and successfully reviewed by the lenders set-up department. It's important to discuss with your AE the lender specific policies concerning TRID. Keep in mind, it's the lender's disclosures that count when maintaining compliance with TRID, not the brokers. If the file was submitted and turned down by another lender, the disclosures from the original lender should be used to maintain compliance. Again, talk to your AE about lender specific policies.

Compensation

Robert Kiyosaki, the best-selling author of *Rich Dad, Poor Dad* once said, "Money does not make you happy, but the lack of money can cause unhappiness." Oh boy, isn't that the truth. As I've mentioned over and over again, the central theme of *An Insiders Guide To Non-QM* is to help mortgage brokers and mortgage loan originators make money. It's why we're all here and what gets us up in the morning. The timing of this book is precarious due to the fact that, not too long ago, non-QM lenders only offered borrower paid compensation. As the non-QM products have evolved, some lenders have started offering lender-paid compensation. I'll explain both. It's important to note that both Dodd-Frank and Regulation Z prohibit basing a loan originator's compensation on the terms of the transaction. More specifically, it prohibits increasing the interest rate. In addition, the loan originator may receive compensation from either the borrower or the lender, but not from both.

Lender Paid Compensation: With lender-paid compensation, the lender and broker agree beforehand on a percentage of the gross loan amount the mortgage loan originator will receive as compensation upon the closing of a loan. This percentage, in most cases, will be between zero and three percent. If the loan being originated is a business purpose loan, the mortgage loan originator can make more. There's no such thing as a free lunch and this is especially the case in the mortgage industry. Compensation paid by the lender is "baked" into the rate. In other words, a mortgage with lender paid compensation will come with a higher than market interest rate (all else being equal). Many loan originators opt for lender-paid compensation as a means to keep borrowers out of pocket costs low.

Borrower Paid Compensation: In the case of borrower paid compensation, the borrower (instead of the lender) pays the loan originator's commission. The benefit is the borrower is allowed to negotiate the loan originator's fee for services. Additionally, because it's not "baked" into the interest rate, the rate is better than the lender paid option. The downside is the borrower's out of pocket expense is higher.

It's important to remember the employees who worked on the failed clinical trials as discussed earlier. The employees that didn't respond in time, didn't complete paperwork properly, or didn't submit documentation in a timely manner are employees who made a salary. Even though the errors cost their companies millions in lost revenue, they continue to get paid. You and me, we don't receive a salary—we earn our paychecks by closing loans! If a loan doesn't close then we don't make any money. One of the best ways to ensure your loan closes is to submit it correctly. Follow the directions and provide the requested documents in a neat, clean, and organized manner.

Chapter Eight

Non-Qualified Mortgage Lenders and Technology

William T. Woods, an official at the General Accounting Office, says HealthCare.gov, a federal website charged with managing new individual health plans, was marred by inadequate oversight from the Department of Health and Human Services. Woods stated (Pickert) that the Centers for Medicare and Medicaid Services (CMS) "undertook the development of HealthCare.gov without effective planning or oversight practices." According to Woods' testimony, the cost of building one part of HealthCare.gov increased from $56 million to more than $209 million within a three year period. Other expenses increased from $30 million to $85 million. Woods says that by March 2014 CMS obligated $840 million for the development of HealthCare.gov and its supporting systems. To date, estimates produced by Bloomberg Government put the cost of HealthCare.gov at $2.1 billion and rising.

After the market crash of 2007 I worked for a company that was one of the first lenders to again offer loans to borrowers with FICO scores as low as 550. These were not non-QM loans, but similar. The experiment lasted about a year before the company went back to offering a conventional product line. What I observed was a technical and systematic disconnect. The lender I worked for was manually underwriting non-QM type loans, and using a loan origination system (LOS) designed around automated underwriting systems like DU or LP. I referred to the process as a merry-go-round. You submit conditions, and because the loans are more complicated the conditions tended to be more involved. The conditions are organized by computers or an employee with limited experience. The underwriter reviews the loan and signs off half of the conditions. The broker calls, mad as hell, and wants to know why the remaining conditions weren't signed off. The broker again provides conditions and they end up back in the same spot–buried a mile deep in a computer folder the underwriter has no idea exists. The file comes out of underwriting, the conditions still aren't signed off on, and then the process starts all over again.

Non-QM loans can be complex and (for now) need to be underwritten manually. The prequalification process is a manual one because we don't run it through DU or LP. The submission is a manual process. This is mostly to avoid submitting a document that's not required and could be detrimental. Scenarios are not black and white and loans need to be manually underwritten due to extenuating circumstances.

Some things can be automated, but proceed with caution. I like to manually price my loans; however, pricing engines have been adopted by most non-QM lenders. I can tell you from experience, people are smart and very quickly they learn how to manipulate the parameters of the pricing engine to get the best rate possible. This can be troubling when an incorrect rate has been communicated to the borrower. In addition, a manipulated rate produced by a pricing engine can be used to unfairly pit lenders against each other. These practices are eventually exposed, but they sure can cause a headache.

Non-QM lenders tend to be smaller companies and do not have the luxury of an unlimited amount of funds, as was the case for HealthCare.gov. In the private sector, we have owners and investors to report to. A financial return is expected on money invested in technology. Because of this, no one is interested in becoming a technical pioneer in the non-QM space since great sums of money is not expected at this early stage. As any astute entrepreneur will tell you, pioneers tend to get arrows in their back. For now, embrace the manual process of non-QM lenders. It's what's putting your borrower in a new home.

Chapter Nine

Get Out and Get Loans!

In 1900, Robert Baden-Powell became a national hero in Britain for his 219-day defense of Mafeking, South Africa–which lies on the Northern tip. Besides being a war hero, Baden-Powell was also an author and wrote a field manual for British soldiers called *Aids to Scouting*. The book eventually caught on with boys who loved the lessons on tracking and observation, and would organize elaborate games using the book. Hearing this, Baden-Powell decided to write a non-military field manual for adolescents that also emphasized the importance of morality and good deeds. On July 25, 1907, Baden-Powell took a diverse group of adolescents to an island where they set up camp. He taught the boys about camping, observation, deduction, watercraft, life-saving techniques, patriotism, and chivalry. Afterward, Baden-Powell set up a central office which registered new boys and designed a uniform. Baden-Powell's organization would henceforth be known as the Boy Scouts. Their motto is, “Be prepared.”

The motto of the Boy Scouts is simple but powerful. To be prepared means you’re always in a state of readiness, both in mind and body, to do your duty. There are no shortcuts. Like the Boy Scouts, there are no shortcuts to be a successful mortgage loan originator. It’s hard work and you must be prepared. This book has given you the core knowledge, but now come the cold calls, sales visits, and presentations. In this chapter, I will share what I’ve observed from my most successful clients.

Greatest Potential Source of Income

In my experience, the greatest demand in non-QM lending is bank statements as income for the self-employed. The second greatest demand comes from investors looking to purchase or refinance an investment property using a debt service coverage ratio (DSCR) program. Again, another form of self-employment. As a reminder, DSCR uses the property’s cash-flow to income qualify for the loan. If the greatest source of potential income is the self-employed borrower, how do you locate them? I recommend contacting accountants, tax preparers, and lawyers who specialize in bankruptcies or creating corporations. Keep in mind it is illegal to pay referral fees or kickbacks for leads.

Customer Service Management Tool (CRM)

Use a CRM. This system helps to organize your customer's contact information and keep it up to date. It can track interactions and manage accounts. It's designed to help improve the relationship with your customers, and in turn increase the value of a customer.

A CRM works great for me because I can determine how many phone calls I've made, emails I've sent, loans I've submitted, and a lot of other things. I can compare my current month's numbers with the prior month to ensure I'm working just as hard or harder. I understand that a CRM is not conducive to every personality type, but many of the features can be automated and the benefits far outweigh the effort involved. I use Hubspot and I love it. Keep in mind, many CRMs have a free version that's often very robust. Do a google search for "free online CRM."

Marketing List

In the old days, creating a marketing list meant going into the phone book and tearing out the page you needed. Nowadays, things are a lot easier. You can buy a list of course, but that costs money. I have a better way and it's free. Go to your local library and use their ReferrenceUSA subscription. ReferenceUSA is the leading source for business and residential data in the United States. To organize their data they use the North American Industry Classification System (NAICS). NAICS classifies business establishments for the purpose of collecting, analyzing, and publishing statistical data related to the U.S. economy. The NAICS industry codes define establishments based on the activities in which they are primarily engaged. The NAICS codes for accounting firms and tax preparers is 541200. The code for lawyers is 541110. From experience, I know you can download the list in an Excel file format. Do so and use that list to populate your CRM. No, you don't have to enter the information by hand, you can usually upload the list all at one time.

Elevator Pitch

Before you start calling, come up with an elevator pitch. You need an elevator pitch and it should not take you more than thirty seconds to communicate it. Once you have your elevator pitch you should learn it, love it, and live it. I'm always having to develop an elevator pitch. When I do, I say it over and over again until I have it memorized. I'll say a pitch 100 times or more, until I have it just right. Here's the thing when making calls: most of the time no one will pick up. In that instance, leave your elevator pitch as the message along with a return number. If someone does pick up, introduce your self and jump right into your elevator pitch. Either way, you're using your pitch.

You know what I know about non-QM. Let's recap. Non-QM is going to double or triple soon. You know how and why non-QM loans are offered in the marketplace, what types of lenders offer non-QM mortgage loans, and how to choose the best lender and AE for you and your company. In addition, you know what products are offered in the non-QM marketplace, the general guidelines most lenders adhere to, and what's needed to submit a loan to underwriting. Lastly, you have an outline to build a non-QM pipeline. Now it's up to you. Good luck. If you have any additional questions you can send me an email or give me a call.

References

Ahmad, Ali. "MBA Forecasts Purchase Originations to Increase to $1.2 Trillion in 2018." 24 October 2017. *www.mba.org.* Web. January 2018.

Feingold, Spencer. "Lion mauls woman to death at popular South African wildlife sanctuar." 2 March 2018. *CNN.* Web.

Gaffney, Jacob. "S&P: We expect non-QM market to double, or even triple, in size in 2018." 18 January 2018. *HousingWire.com.* Web. <HousingWire.com/articles/42000-sp-we-expect-non-qm-market-to-double-or-even-triple-in-size-in-2018>.

Kenny, Peter. "Lewis Smashes Ruddock in Two." 31 October 1992. *www.upi.com.* Web.

Pickert, Kate. "Report: Cost of Healthcare.gov Approaching $1 Billion." 30 July 2014. *Time.com.* Web.

PK. "The 30 Year Mortgage and Housing Accessibility." Unkown Unkown Unkown. *dqydj.com.*

"The Great Recession." Unknow Day Unknow Month Unknow Year. *investopedia.com.* Web.

Thebritishmuseum.org. Unknow Day Unknow Month Unknow Year. Web.

Wikipedia Contributors. "French campaign in Egypt and Syria." 5 April 2018. *Wikipedia, The Free Encyclopedia.* Web.

http://non-qminsider.com

—. "Morgage Bankers Association." 18 March 2018. *Wikpedia, The Free Encyclopedia.* Web.

Your Voice is Important.

I appreciate hearing from you. Please leave a helpful review on **Amazon**. Let me know what was useful and what can make this book even better.

Your feedback is invaluable for the next edition of this book!

Loan Scenarios

To discuss loan scenarios please visit www.non-qminsider.com and click on "loan scenario" in the upper right hand corner. There you will be able to submit questions concerning a specific loan scenario you currently have.

Made in United States
North Haven, CT
04 November 2026

21768338R00048